AUSTRALIA

in pictures

Prepared by Jo McDonald

The uncrowned King of Australia.

**VISUAL
GEOGRAPHY
SERIES**

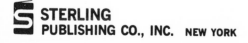

**STERLING
PUBLISHING CO., INC.** NEW YORK

Oak Tree Press Co., Ltd.
Distributed by WARD LOCK, Ltd.
London & Sydney

VISUAL GEOGRAPHY SERIES

A pleasure boat cruises down the Derwent River in Tasmania.

NOTE

The dollars mentioned in this book are the new Australian dollars. Australian decimal currency, effective since February, 1966.

PICTURE CREDITS

The publishers wish to thank the following for the use of the photographs and maps in this book: Australian News & Information Bureau, Canberra; Australian News & Information Bureau, London; Australian News & Information Bureau, New York; News & Information Bureau, Australian Department of the Interior; and the United Nations.

Seventh Printing, 1971
Copyright © 1970, 1969, 1968, 1966 by
Sterling Publishing Co., Inc.
419 Park Avenue South, New York, N.Y. 10016
British edition published by Oak Tree Press Co., Ltd.
Distributed in Great Britain and the Commonwealth by
Ward Lock, Ltd., 116 Baker Street, London W1
Manufactured in the United States of America
All rights reserved
Library of Congress Catalog Card No.: 66-16198
ISBN 0-8069-1040-2   UK 7061 6002 9
1041-0

An aborigine stockman and his horse take a break at a stockyard east of Darwin.

CONTENTS

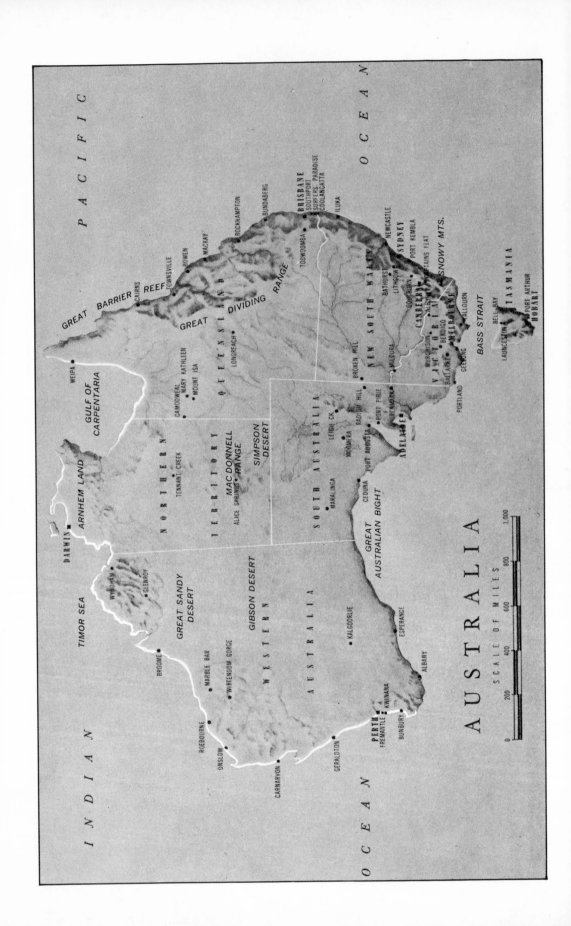

"The Founding of Australia" depicts the unfurling of the British flag at Sydney Cove on January 26, 1788, now celebrated as Australia Day. Captain Arthur Phillip, his officers and guard of marines are about to drink the health of King George III. In this painting by Algernon Talmage, R.A., their brig *"Supply"* is seen anchored in the cove.

I. HISTORY

A GREAT TRACT of land had to exist, the old map makers thought, in the Southern Hemisphere, to balance the land-masses in the north, so they marked this empty space, *Terra Australis Incognita*—the Unknown Land of the South.

DISCOVERY

Chinese and Malay navigators probably visited the shores of this land with the Spanish and the Portuguese. Certainly the Dutch came sailing down the northern coast: Willem Jansz aboard the yacht "Duyfken" in 1606; Dirk Hartog landed on the west coast in 1616, and in 1642 Abel Tasman, on a trading and exploring voyage, discovered the island Van Diemen's Land, now called Tasmania, and New Zealand. Tasman, repulsed by hostile natives, sailed back for Holland and thus ended Dutch exploration in the area.

In 1688, the English buccaneer William Dampier, aboard the "Roebuck," explored the

An early picture of Sydney as it looked a few years after the founding of the Colony. Captain Phillip was the first Governor of New South Wales and his Government House was originally a canvas tent. Following the American Revolution it was no longer possible for Britain to send its overflowing prison population to the New World, so along with free settlers to Australia came the first convicts who were landed at Botany Bay near Sydney.

northwest coast, but all these navigators reported arid and inhospitable shores and it remained for Captain James Cook, in 1770, who charted the east coast, to take possession of the land in the name of Britain.

The word, "Australia," meaning South Land, was first used by still another English navigator, Matthew Flinders, who surveyed the coastlines between 1795 and 1803. Up till then this great tract of land was known by its Dutch name, New Holland, or Botany Bay.

We must go back a few years to Britain's American colonies and their War of Independence against George III. After this took place, somewhere else had to be found to send the overflow of transported offenders from England's prisons, and on January 18–20, 1788, the First Fleet of eleven ships under the command of Captain Arthur Phillip landed at Botany Bay, after an 8-month voyage from England.

The First Fleet brought 1,000 souls to this new land—convicts, their marine guards and officers. Eight days later, the little settlement

The bronze statue of Captain Charles Sturt, the famous explorer, in Queen Victoria Square, Adelaide. Sturt explored the river system of South Australia and discovered the Darling River in 1828. Later he became Colonial Secretary.

The Guard Towers and walls are the last remains of the old convict settlement at Port Arthur. It was founded in 1830 when Tasmania was still called Van Diemen's Land. The well known book by Marcus Clarke, "For The Term of His Natural Life," was set here. Transportation to Tasmania was abolished in 1853.

moved from Botany Bay to Port Jackson, at the mouth of Sydney Cove, and Captain Phillip, in command of the garrison, became Australia's first Governor.

In spite of early difficulties with lack of supplies and farming skills, the settlement grew and some land was cultivated. But the crops were poor and the resourceful Captain Phillip set off to look for better agricultural land. He discovered the Hawkesbury River with its fertile belt, then went inland to the Blue Mountains, part of the Great Dividing

Growing along the inaccessible walls of the old prison at Port Arthur is a scarlet flower called "Kiss-Me-Quick" which is identical with the "Fire Flower" that appeared in the ruins of London after the Great Fire of 1666, and again after the bombing in 1941.

Now in ruins, the church at Port Arthur, Tasmania, patterned after Glastonbury Abbey in England, is thought to have been built by a convict named Mason who was given a free pardon for his work. Local freestone was used. Built in 1836, it was designed to accommodate 1,000 worshippers and to be open to all faiths.

Range which separated the coastal slopes from the interior.

By now the early colonists were facing great difficulties. Sometimes it was months between rains. The soft English wheat died, cattle sickened or escaped into the bush, supply ships were delayed or lost, and the infant colony was on starvation rations before these first problems were overcome.

Then in 1813 three men found a way through the Blue Mountains: George Blaxland, an experienced English farmer, the Army Lieutenant William Lawson, who was also interested in agriculture, and William Wentworth, who was the acting provost marshal; and it was they who found the pasture lands stretching westward to the horizon.

EXPLORATION

In the wake of these first explorers, John Oxley, a former naval officer who had been appointed surveyor-general, and George Evans, the deputy surveyor-general, explored the Macquarie and the Lachlan Rivers.

Hamilton Hume, the son of the agricultural instructor of the convicts, William Howell, and the botanist, Allan Cunningham, journeyed overland to the Southern Ocean. Cunningham then went northward and found the rich Darling Downs of Queensland.

It was Captain Charles Sturt, whose regiment had come to Australia in 1827, who traced the course of several rivers running inland from the coastal mountains. He discovered the Darling, and the following year took a whaleboat down the Murrumbidgee until it flowed into the Murray River, following it out, after great hardships, through Lake Alexandrina, to the sea.

In 1844, Edward Eyre led a party northward in an attempt to reach the heart of Australia, but in the face of an unusually severe drought, he had to turn back before reaching the Tropic of Capricorn.

Ludwig Leichhardt, a German naturalist, made his way from the Darling Downs to Darwin. In a later expedition, in an attempt to cross the continent from east to west, Leichhardt and his party disappeared in the "never-never" lands of the interior and their fate still remains a mystery.

Meanwhile, a second settlement had been established at Hobart in Tasmania, a third on the Brisbane River, and a fourth on the Swan River in Western Australia.

Other expeditions followed, made by men whose names still ring in Australian history: Major Thomas Mitchell, Edmund Kennedy, the Gregory Brothers, John Stuart, Robert Burke, a police inspector, and William Wills, an astronomer, who both lost their lives in the bush; Angus McMillan, a cattle hand, and the Polish count, Paul de Strzelecki, who crossed eastern Victoria together.

Settlements, later to develop into colonies, then into States, followed the discoveries of these explorers.

Coal was discovered in 1796 at Newcastle, named after the English city, Newcastle-upon-Tyne. Colliers, plying between Newcastle and Sydney were called "Sixty-Milers," since that was the distance. "Thistle," a paddle steamer with sails, passes her sister ship "Rose," both famous Sixty-Milers.

The interior of Australia, the bush, is also called the outback or the Never-Never. Here, crossing the dry bed of the Diamantina River in Queensland, come supplies for a lonely station.

DEVELOPMENT

The early Governors had the power to make free land grants to anyone—emancipated prisoners, new settlers, marines and officers of the garrison—who would employ the convicts and take over from the Administration the task of feeding and clothing them.

With the rapid growth of a free population and with more stock, the original settlements spread, and following on the heels of those early explorers, there was an overflow into the western plains.

Ownership of land was established by occupation or "squatting," hence squatters or land-owners.

Before 1800, Captain John Macarthur, an officer in The New South Wales Corps, had begun experiments in sheep breeding. A boat-load of Spanish merinos, sent to Africa's Cape Province, had been considered too odd-looking to land there and were shipped, most fortunately, on to Australia. These, bred with sheep from the Royal Flocks in England, gave Australia the basis of its enormous wool industry. By 1810, the Spanish merino was turned into a superb wool-bearing animal and the coastal strip of New South Wales supported 25,000 sheep.

With migration and natural increase of population, transportation of convicts was moved to the newly settled Western Australia which was now in vital need of manpower.

Leviathan, a fully loaded stage coach, drawn by 8 horses, sets off from a Sydney hotel in an early picture of the Colony.

Sydney seen from the air shows the many bays and inlets of its port, with the bridge. In the distance facing the Pacific Ocean are Bondi and Coogee Beaches.

Gold was discovered in 1851 at Bathurst on the Western plains of New South Wales and brought a great influx of men to Australia from all over the world. Soon after that, rich reefs were found at Ballarat in Victoria, then at Bendigo—the three golden B's which boosted the population from 400,000 to 1,400,000 in ten years and unearthed £106,000,000 (British) in gold.

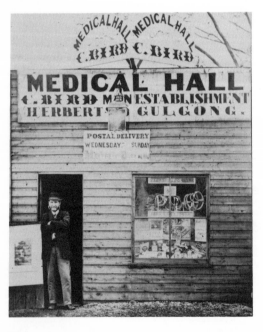

THE GOLD RUSH

From 1788 to 1868, 155,000 convicts were transported to Australia from Britain. In 1851, when the development of the colonies was almost at a standstill, Edward Hargraves discovered gold at Bathurst in New South Wales, and this brought a new influx of free migrants to Australia.

Richer finds were made at Ballarat in Victoria, then at Bendigo. When the gold had been worked out, interest was turned to farming and grazing. Even greater deposits were discovered at Kalgoorlie, in Western Australia, where gold

Gulgong also had Matthew the Bellman, the Town Crier and postman, seen here stationed outside the combined post office and pharmacy.

Gulgong, a typical goldrush town in the 1870's, boasts a newspaper office (above) with the hairdresser, in white, and the town dandy holding his cane.

was actually broken off outcropping rocks in lumps.

The discovery of gold influenced the country in other ways, since it brought to Australia people of widely different occupations and this new blood had far-reaching effects.

Adventurous prospectors were enticed inland. New finds were made. Tradesmen followed, then roads and railways. Many who had sought gold unsuccessfully, turned to farming and manufacturing. Others went still farther inland.

With this new interest in the land, men began to experiment with seeds and farming instruments suitable to Australian conditions. Secondary industry followed. Church schools and universities were founded and the framework for free education for all children was established.

Australia, in a very few years, had come of age.

The undertaker, in his bark-walled premises, also undertakes to build, do cabinet work and carpentry as well as bury the good people of Gulgong.

The world's first Ski Club was formed at Kiandra in the Australian Alps by Norwegian "diggers" who had arrived in 1860 for the gold rush. Originally known as the "Snow-Shoe Club," the Kiandra miners evolved their own type of skis, the binding being a leather band into which they kicked their boots. They skied with feet wide apart and carried a single brake pole on which they sat to steady themselves downhill.

Hill End in New South Wales was a boom town in the 1870's and J. Kennedy found it worth-while to move his small tailoring business from Sydney.

(Above) When the gold miners sent for their wives and children, the first houses in Gulgong were built of wattle-and-daub with bark roofs, and when a miner struck it rich he moved his family into a new frame house (below).

Ayers Rock, in the Northern Territory, one of the largest single rocks in the world, is dark red (especially red at sunset) and is sacred to the aborigines. In their legends it is associated with "Dream Time" (Creation). The rock rises 1,000 feet above the surrounding plain and is a mile wide.

2. THE LAND

AUSTRALIA is the world's only continent inhabited by a single people. It lies in the southern hemisphere between the Pacific and the Indian Oceans and occupies 3,000,000 square miles. Completely bounded by sea, its coastline exceeds 12,000 miles. Separated from the mother country, England, by 9,537 sea miles, the country is 400 miles from the closest Asian outpost—the island of Timor to the north. Australia's "relative," New Zealand, lies 1,200 miles to the southeast at its nearest point.

Australia, about the size of the continental United States, is the smallest and the flattest of the continents. Most of it is one vast ancient crustal block, the Western Plateau, about 1,000 feet above sea level. Another large portion is the Central-Eastern Lowlands, which formed the beds of ancient seas. The third division is the Eastern Highlands, the Great Dividing Range, with Mt. Kosciusko its highest peak (7,314 ft.), running north and south along the eastern boundary.

The Bottle or Gourd-Gourd Tree grows in Northern Australia. In the hollows formed at the base of the branches many gallons of good, sweet water are stored by the tree for the dry season. This water is used by roving aborigines, birds and other travellers.

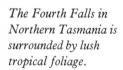

The Fourth Falls in Northern Tasmania is surrounded by lush tropical foliage.

Drought is the worst enemy of cattle in the Northern Territory. Although drinking water is available from artesian basins, lack of rain has reduced this station at Love's Creek to a desert.

WATER

Australia has two great shortages, men and water. It lacks river systems in the dry interior and the Murray River, the country's greatest, fed by the Darling, the Lachlan and the Murrumbidgee, has, until very recently, been pouring all of its fresh water into the sea.

Most of the interior rivers flow only after heavy rains, then dry up to a few water-holes, although artesian water has now been proved over one third of the continent.

The eastern mountain chain, or Great Dividing Range, contains most of the forests.

This farmer is crop spraying with insecticide at "Glencoe," Wee Waa, New South Wales, which is becoming the cotton bowl of Australia.

The Snowy Mountains Hydro-Electric Scheme, by damming water from three rivers, the Snowy, the Murray and the Murrumbidgee, will provide 2,000,000 acre feet of irrigation water each year. Valuable fresh water which formerly flowed eastward into the sea is now diverted inland by long tunnels through the mountains to join the western rivers. The diverted water generates electricity as it passes through the turbines of several large power stations. This view shows the Guthega Dam.

Work on the long Eucumbene Diversion Tunnel.

The coastal plains, built up of soil washed down from the mountains, are the most fertile areas and most of the population has settled here. Round the Murray River and its tributaries citrus fruit, soft fruit and wheat are grown. In the uplands are the great sheep runs.

To conserve the precious water of these rivers for agriculture west of the Great Divide, the Snowy Mountain Scheme came into being and is one of the world's largest irrigation and power projects. The Snowy River, with its source on the eastern slopes of the Divide, originally flowed into the Tasman Sea. West of the Divide, the Murrumbidgee and the Murray flow through fertile plains which have a low rainfall, and these are the plains to be irrigated by the new Scheme.

Diverting the water of the Snowy River into tunnels through the mountains is Part II of the Scheme. Part I is the diversion of the Eucumbene River, a tributary of the Snowy, by way of the Tumut River into the Murrumbidgee. New hydro-electric power stations are designed to utilize the 2,600-foot fall of water from the Snowy to the Murray and will supply 50 per cent of Australia's present generating capacity.

The diverted water will irrigate 1,000 square miles in the two dry river valleys and supply South Australia during the drought periods.

Capital required for construction work is 800,000,000 Australian dollars, provided by the Federal Government on loan. The Snowy Mountain Scheme will be finished by 1975.

The Tumut 2 Power Station is 800 feet underground.

STATES AND TERRITORIES

Working clockwise round Australia, we begin at 4 o'clock with New South Wales or Botany Bay, the first State to be settled, and here the map will be of help.

Sydney, the capital, is built on a sea inlet which spreads inland for 21 miles with a network of small inlets and bays. North of Sydney is Newcastle, a busy industrial city, where coal was discovered. Inland are Bathurst, where the Gold Rush began, and Broken Hill, where silver was first mined. New South Wales produces nearly 50 per cent of the Australian output of wool.

At 4:30 our clock hand brings us to Canberra, Australian Capital Territory and the seat of the Commonwealth Government. It is from here that the whole continent is administered. This is the home of the Governor-General and of all the overseas embassies and legations.

Five o'clock brings us to Victoria, the smallest and most closely settled of the mainland States. Melbourne, its capital on the River Yarra, has a rising population of 2,000,000. Among these are many new migrants who have brought fresh blood and vitality to the city. Ballarat and Bendigo, the two inland cities, began as gold mining towns.

Across the Bass Strait, at 5:30 on our clock, we have the island State of Tasmania, with Hobart, the capital, set on the Derwent River.

21

The unusual El Alamein Fountain in Sydney's Kings Cross area is a cool place round which to relax and meet friends.

Sydney, capital of New South Wales, is the oldest city in Australia. Circular Quay was the site of the first British settlement in 1788. It is now the ferry terminal.

Oarsmen ply the Yarra River in Melbourne at sundown. Melbourne, growing nearly as fast as Sydney, has an interesting past. Known as Dootigala (Douta Galla) when it was settled in 1837, it was re-named after Lord Melbourne, Queen Victoria's Prime Minister.

Adelaide, the capital of South Australia, is the most beautifully designed of the Australian cities. Laid out by the first Surveyor-General, Colonel William Light, soon after the establishment of the Colony in 1836, it is situated on the banks of the Torrens River half-way between the Mount Lofty Ranges and the seacoast at St. Vincent's Gulf. The heart of the city is one mile square, bounded on four sides by wide terraces and further separated from its suburbs by a green belt of parklands.

Perth, the capital of Western Australia, was founded in 1829 on the estuary of the Swan River. Its port is Fremantle on the Indian Ocean, the first port of call for ships from Europe, India and Africa.

Hobart is the capital of Tasmania, the island separated from the mainland of Australia by Bass Strait. Constitution Dock, seen here, is the picturesque, deep-water port for a large fishing fleet, 12 miles inland from the Derwent Estuary. Behind the city is snow-capped Mount Wellington.

This mountainous little island has the most varied scenery in Australia: lakes, cascades, steeply falling rivers, and above all, stone houses. Many of the first English craftsmen who came here built in stone in memory of home, and Tasmania, with its apple orchards and grazing cattle, is the most English in appearance and climate of the six States.

At 6 o'clock we come to South Australia with Adelaide, the capital city, sheltered by the Mount Lofty Ranges. Wheat, wool, wine and ship-building are the main industries. Iron Knob, a mountain of iron ore, supplies the blast furnaces of Whyalla. In the semi-arid desert to the north is the weapons testing range of Woomera. Seaward is the Great Australian Bight.

At 7 o'clock we cross the vast Nullarbor Plain to Western Australia, the largest of the States, with Perth, its capital city on the Indian Ocean. Western Australia is called by its own people the "Western Third" since it constitutes one third of Australia's land-mass. Close to Perth is Fremantle, the main port for ships from Europe and India. Kalgoorlie goldfields are still the most productive in Australia, but the new wealth of the State lies in the vast wheat-growing areas at Esperance, cotton crops at the Ord River where many Arizona farmers have brought their experience to bear, and the booming iron deposits at Pilboa and Koolyanobbing. In the interior of Western Australia are the Gibson and the Great Sandy Deserts.

Two other ports in this sparsely populated State are Port Hedland and Broome where the famous pearl, "Star of the West," was found.

Canberra's streets shine on a rainy night. Australian Capital Territory, 900 square miles, houses the seat of the Government of the Commonwealth.

A ship is unloaded at the new wharf at Darwin. Dockworkers wear the typical Australian dress, shorts, shirt and a wide-brimmed hat.

Here, too, in the north are the aborigine reservations.

Twelve o'clock brings us to the Northern Territory, which is not one of the six States, but a separate territory administered by the Federal Government in Canberra. Darwin, its capital, is named after Charles Darwin, the English naturalist who was aboard the "Beagle" when she sailed through the Timor Sea and landed there.

Most of the Northern Territory is dry desert and tableland with cattle stations—Alexandra Downs, the largest is 11,262 square miles. Recently, the discovery of manganese in Arnhem

The Sisters Islands lie off the northwest coast, the farmlands of Tasmania. In the south are the apple orchards from which the island gets its pet name, "Apple Isle."

Alice Springs, once a tiny township lost in the Never-Never of the Northern Territory, has blossomed into the main railhead town of central Australia. Alice Springs is set among the stark hills of the MacDonnell Range and is the collecting point for cattle from the vast properties to the north.

Land and uranium at Rum Jungle brought new wealth to the Territory. Alice Springs, connected with Darwin by the Stuart Highway, is in the very heart of Australia. Not too far off is Ayers Rock, "the largest red pebble in the world."

One o'clock takes us across the Gulf of Carpentaria to the Territories of Papua and

Cattle being mustered at Jay Creek, an aboriginal welfare station near Alice Springs in central Australia.

Cattle in a holding yard in the Gulf country, south of the Gulf of Carpentaria, where the first European ship, the Dutch yacht "Duyfken," landed in 1606.

A Merino sheep breaks loose after being landed in New Guinea. Papua and New Guinea are both territories administered by Australia, together with Norfolk and Christmas Islands, Nauru and the Cocos Islands.

The Brisbane River divides Brisbane, the capital of Queensland, from its suburbs. The city was settled in 1824 and now exports textiles, wool, meat, gold and sugar. Many recent immigrants from Italy have settled in Queensland to work in the cane fields. Queensland's fine natural resources and climate offer excellent potential for growth.

New Guinea, administered by Australia under a trusteeship.

Most of the 2,000,000 people here, and in the surrounding islands, Melanesians, Negritos and Papuans, live in scattered villages pursuing their traditional way of life; the terrain, jungle growth and mountains making communication difficult and development slow. The chief products are copra, rubber and coffee. Port Moresby is the capital and the seat of administration for these Territories.

Two o'clock on our clock brings us to Queensland, the sixth State, with Brisbane its capital city, on the Pacific Ocean.

A stockman holding stud cattle for inspection at Bluff Downs in northern Queensland.

The Great Barrier Reef in the Coral Sea runs for 1,250 miles down the Queensland coast, and is the longest coral reef in the world. It forms a natural breakwater for the coast and contains innumerable islets with coral gardens and the most varied marine life. This picture was taken from the Whitsunday Islands.

To the north near Townsville we have one of the most beautiful tropical coastlines in the world, and the Great Barrier Reef, a huge wall of coral.

Behind, on the coastal slopes and river flats are cane fields, pineapple, paw-paw, mango and tobacco. Further inland on the rolling plains we find wheat, cattle and sheep.

Mineral deposits include copper, lead and zinc at Mount Isa, bauxite at Weipa and uranium at Mary Kathleen. Queensland also possesses Australia's first proved oilfield at Moonie. Other coastal cities are Cairns,

(Left) Butterfly cod swim through their coral gardens. They can be viewed through portholes of the underwater observatory at Green Island.

Snow-coated Mount Kosciusko (7,314 ft.) in the Australian Alps in southeastern New South Wales is the highest point in Australia. The peak was discovered by the Polish explorer Paul de Strzelecki who named it after a great Polish hero—General Thaddeús Kosciusko who fought in the American Revolution.

Rockhampton and Gladstone. South of Brisbane lies the Gold Coast with its miles of surfing beaches.

At 4 o'clock our hand has brought us round to New South Wales and Botany Bay, our starting point. Four o'clock is also tea-time and the Australians, after the Russians, are the greatest tea drinkers on earth.

Kings Cross, the most thickly populated district in Sydney, is also the Latin quarter. Because of the good climate, dining in café terraces is becoming increasingly popular. Writers, poets, painters and larrikins gravitate to Kings Cross (larrikin, an old Cornish word, means a street tough); visitors flock to its restaurants and nightclubs.

Since 1947, Australia has established three research stations in her Antarctic Territory: Heard Island, Macquerie Island and Mawson. "Kista Dan," the Danish icebreaker, is seen wedged in the sea ice on her 12,000-mile voyage to visit all three stations.

Time for a halt. A pyramid tent is put up by an exploring party.

King William Saddle in Tasmania invites you to leave the shade of the gums.

CLIMATE

The Australian climate, although varied because of the very size of the continent, has no great extremes. In the north above the Tropic of Capricorn, it is generally tropical with the temperature ranging from 75° F. to over 85° F. In the arid plateaus and deserts of the interior, there are hot days and cold nights. The southern states and Tasmania are in the temperate zone with temperatures falling below 45° F.

FLORA

Australia's long isolation as a land-mass has resulted in flora peculiar to itself. The arid conditions and porous soils have led to the development of plant life capable of withstanding drought, with eucalyptus trees and wattles (acacia) predominating. The eucalyptus or gum tree has 500 species and can be found growing in all but the waterless desert. The yellow wattle has found its place on the Australian coat-of-arms.

A new bungalow nestles under the shade of a gum tree in a suburb of Canberra.

The kookaburra, a member of the kingfisher family, has been called the Bushman's Clock because of his infectious laugh at sunrise and sunset. Perched on a branch he throws his head back and gives a gay full-throated laugh.

FAUNA

The severance of land bridges with other continents left Australia as an island sanctuary for its large population of marsupials—animals which carry their young in a pouch, like the kangaroo and the wallaby. The koala or tree bear belongs, zoologists think, to the same family as the American ring-tailed possum.

The dingo, a member of the dog family, is now thought to be descended from a domesticated version of the Asiatic wolf that accompanied the ancestors of the Australian aborigines on their early migrations by sea and then ran wild.

The duck-billed platypus, a furred creature which lays eggs, represents a stage of evolution from the reptile to the mammal. It suckles its young, has webbed feet, dives into the muddy beds of rivers, searching, as a duck does, for food, and builds its nest in burrows on the banks.

A dinkum Aussie—this Weddell seal is one of the rare inhabitants encountered on a long sledge trip through Australia's coldest territory.

The koala, or "native bear," dozes in a gum tree. He sleeps in the daytime and lives on eucalyptus leaves.

The duck-billed platypus uses his snout to catch food. His powerful claws enable him to burrow into river banks to nest.

The Australian birds range from the giant emu which cannot fly, to the black swan of the west; the glorious tailed lyrebird which can mimic the songs of other birds; the bower bird, that builds "playhalls" or "bowers" for its elaborate courtship dances; the brolga, a member of the crane family that also dances; the parrot; the cockatoo; the budgerigar, or love bird; and the laughing kookaburra.

Australia is well aware that in the not-too-distant future it will undoubtedly be faced with the problem of how to preserve its unique native wildlife. Already, as settlement spreads across the country, animals such as the kangaroo, which are heavy grass eaters, are being

Mother is a great grey kangaroo. In her pouch, almost ready to face the world, is a "joey." The baby might grow seven feet tall and become an old man kangaroo.

The dingo is the wild dog of Australia. Sandy brown and strongly built, the dingo has roamed the continent for at least 40,000 years.

The emu, Australia's largest bird, like the smaller cassowary, is extremely swift-footed but cannot fly.

The white sulphur-crested cockatoo is found throughout Australia. In captivity, he will respond to "Dance, Cocky!" and move jauntily from one leg to the other on his perch.

A grey kangaroo can reach 30 miles per hour as he makes bounds of 30 feet.

hunted as a threat to the sheep grazing industry. Others, like the koala who barely escaped extinction, his numbers reduced to a few hundred by fur trappers, are now protected by law.

Conservation of wildlife in Australia will be a long and costly project. Although a great many parks now exist, they are not as yet strictly regulated and maintained as preserves.

The Black Swan, found throughout Australia, was discovered by a Dutch expedition under William de Vlamingh in 1697. The Swan River takes its name from these graceful birds. The Black Swan is the emblem of Western Australia.

Manly Beach, seven miles by ferry, is only one of 19 surfing beaches near Sydney.

3. THE PEOPLE

IN ORDER TO UNDERSTAND the Australian character, as distinct from the New Zealand or the Canadian which also have strong ties with Britain, we must go back to the very beginnings of the colony and know how it was first settled.

The War of Independence prevented transportation of convicted persons to America, and in 1779 Sir Joseph Banks suggested to a House of Commons committee that Botany Bay was a suitably remote place to "establish a colony of convicted felons." On May 13, 1787, the First Fleet under Captain Arthur Phillip's command, arrived at Botany Bay on January 18, 1788.

Finding the bay unsuitable, Phillip established the colony at Sydney Cove. Of these early settlers, some of them were political prisoners, some mere poachers or rick-burners, and a great many of them Irish who considered themselves not felons, but patriotic rebels.

This beginning also separated the early Australians into two classes, the *exclusives*, the land-owning squatters and the *emancipists*, the free settlers and their descendants.

The gold rushes after 1851 brought new types of men to Australia, all of whom paid their own high fares in the hope of finding gold; most of these came from the British Isles. In ten years the country's population trebled.

By the twentieth century Australia had become so selective over whom it would

Sydney's George Street in the morning.

welcome to its shores that the "Sydney Bulletin," which formed public opinion more than any other journal, had for its slogan, "Australia for the Australians—The Cheap Chinaman, the Cheap Negro, the Cheap European Pauper to be Absolutely Excluded."

Two world wars have changed the picture considerably, and although still selective, much new blood is being brought into Australia. In 1970, the total population was 12,371,000.

Nevertheless, the country, since 1962, has been experiencing a slump in the birth rate. Experts feel, however, that the picture may well change when the post-World War II babies marry and begin their own families.

A lowering of the population is a matter of national concern to a country as large and sparsely populated as Australia and would have serious economic effects. The Australian government, through the Ministry of Social Services, now offers child endowment payments (baby bonuses) to Australian mothers. In the opinion of some, these payments should be increased to encourage and enable young married people to raise and support larger families.

Francis Adams, the English poet, writing in 1895 on the people of the outback, said:

"Where the marine rainfall flags out and is lost, a new climate and in a certain sense, a new race begins to unfold. It is not a hundred, but three, or four, or five hundred miles that you must go back from the sea if you will find yourself face to face with the one powerful and unique national type yet produced in the new land . . .

"Frankly, I find not only all that is genuinely characteristic of Australia and the Australians from this heart of the land, but all that is noblest, kindliest and best."

The following brief story will illustrate something of the Australian character, which, while owing strong allegiance to the Crown in the person of Queen Elizabeth II, is still unawed.

It took place during the Royal visit to Australia in 1953. It had been a long, hot day and the young Queen was visibly wilting by the time they reached a school for deaf and dumb children. As she took her place on the platform, Prince Philip, her husband, leant over and whispered in her ear. The children present, who could read his lips, broke out with delighted applause. The Queen, realizing what had happened, looked up at her husband and she, too, began to laugh.

He had said: "Cheer up, Little Dumpling."

THE OUTBACK

While the vast, dry interior has strongly affected the Australian outlook, most of the people live on the coastal belts, in the growing

Queen Elizabeth with some of her subjects from the outback. She visited lonely cattle stations and townships between Alice Springs and Darwin on her 1953 tour.

With over 170,000,000 sheep in the whole of Australia a motorcycle helps with the rounding up. The horse is being replaced by the cycle and the drover, when he moves from paddock to paddock, takes his kelpie—sheepdog—with him on the cycle.

Chips Rafferty, the film actor, typifies the bush-ranger, the cattle drover and other men of action from the outback.

cities of Sydney, Melbourne, Brisbane, Adelaide, and Perth, but it will be seen through the following song, the most popular in Australia, how dear the bushman, the man from outback, is to their hearts.

"Once a jolly swagman . . ."

The lines of "Waltzing Matilda" by the bush poet, Banjo Paterson, sums up this feeling well:

Once a jolly swagman
  (a man looking for work, carrying his bedroll)
Camped by a billabong (water-hole)
Under the shade of a coolibah tree (eucalyptus)
And he sang as he watched
And waited while his billy boiled
  (tin can for making tea on a fire)

"You'll come a-waltzing Matilda with me!"
  (waltzing or walking Matilda, the swag)
Down came a jumbuck (sheep)
To drink at the billabong
  (billa—water, bong—dead, two aboriginal
  words)
Up jumped the swagman
And grabbed him with glee,
And he sang as he stowed that
Jumbuck in his tucker-bag (food bag)
"You'll come a-waltzing Matilda with me!"
Up rode the squatter (land-owner)
Mounted on his thoroughbred (fine horse)
Down came the troopers (country police)
One, two, three . . . and so on.

Resentment against the rich squatter who

The billycan boils and the thirsty cane cutters take a break for tea. Mechanical cutting is not general owing to the small size of the holdings. The cane is cut by contract gangs, many of them Italian immigrants, the New Australians. After felling the cane and lopping off the bushy tip, the workers load it on to trucks for transport to the mills.

At Yirrkalla, on the Arnhem Land Aboriginal Reservation in the Northern Territory, men gather to chant the songs of their beliefs. The music is provided by the didjeridoo, a hollow stick eaten out by termites.

held large tracts of land by the man looking for work was well caught in the song, and its continued popularity shows the Australian's strong love of freedom and fair play.

All these new words in "Waltzing Matilda" with others—stockman, shearer, drover, bushwacker, boundary rider—conjure up the life on the great sheep and cattle runs of central Australia where water is scarce and the stock is utterly dependent on the sparse rainfall. Drought is like a spectre always stalking the interior and water is more valuable than gold. It makes, therefore, for a new type of man, the bushman, the man from outback, who can think quickly and live on his wits; one who loves the great, dry stretches of land, the sparse gums, the unending horizon and the welcome sight of the trees and the water tanks of some lonely homestead.

THE ABORIGINES

Another interesting influence on the national character, according to Russel Ward, is the aboriginal.

These primitive, dark-skinned, wavy-haired people, the Australoids, found living here by the first Europeans, were among the most unwarlike tribes known to history. While individuals might be killed for breaking taboos, their "wars" consisted of two tribes meeting at a traditional place, where after exchanging insults and challenges, the men would hurl spears at each other and dodge them with great skill. Prestige and glory having being satisfied they would leave.

Whatever the reasons for the aborigines' unwarlike spirit, there has been singularly little physical violence in Australian life, and Aus-

One returning boomerang is caught as another is thrown. This type is used only for sport. The large war boomerang does not return.

Within these boundaries they led nomadic lives, wandering in search of food, practising no form of agriculture; pitting themselves against their harsh land so steadfastly that they developed amazing skills in tracking, hunting and finding water in order to survive.

They had few possessions and wore no clothes, carrying just a digging stick, a dilly bag for food and a drone pipe. Their weapons were the boomerang, the barbed wooden spear, the stone axe, the trap, the net and the pointed yam stick.

The designs on their weapons were often the sacred symbols of their religious life. Such symbols were held to endow them with power from the spirit world of mystical beings responsible for creation, the traditional heroes; and food killed by such a weapon could only be eaten by fully initiated men.

In their ceremonies the initiate might enter, after the most painful ordeals, into the "dream" life and be in touch with the invisible things of the past, the present and the future. Thought messages could be sent and received; the old men of the tribe being the custodians of all the religious secrets.

tralians have always been extremely slow to shed one another's blood.

When Captain Phillip's colonists landed in 1788, the aborigines probably numbered 300,000. These distinctive people were hunters and food gatherers whose ancestors had migrated from Asia over a period of thousands of years.

They did not build permanent homes. In many places they slept and rested in the open with small fires burning if they needed warmth. Some groups built huts of saplings and mud; most, however, bundled branches together into wurlies (huts) or made primitive lean-to's of bark sheets.

Each one of the 500 tribes recognized each other's tribal area. These were not only places to hunt, but areas where they performed their ceremonies and maintained their social ties.

Jacob, a newly initiated Pintibi lad, with a bamboo spear.

This crayon drawing of a Grass Tree was done by a young aboriginal child from Western Australia.

Far from leading random lives, the aborigines were strictly disciplined by various social ties and by their involved kinship rules. Also the young and hardy were required to provide for the old and feeble.

Yet they were not oppressed with their magic and supernatural powers. Much of their ceremony was singing and dancing to the drone of the didjeridoo.

Today the full-blood aborigines number only 100,000, most of them living in Western Australia and Northern Territory. But instead of wishing to live secluded in their reservations, they are attracted to the white man's world, causing formidable problems of administration and assimilation.

A stockman at Beswick Station paints his didjeridoo for a corroboree.

A broken leg case is carried by stretcher to the ambulance plane.

NEW AUSTRALIANS

While Australia has for many generations drawn its settlers from the British Isles, since 1945 it has welcomed thousands of new settlers, called *New Australians*, from Holland, Germany, Italy, France, Greece, the Baltic countries and the U.S.A. By 1963, 2,000,000 of these New Australians had arrived, half of them under schemes of assisted passage. The national policy of a "White Australia" has been maintained.

FLYING DOCTOR SERVICE

When the people of Australia's lonely inland areas need medical aid they use the radio to call a "flying doctor," and an aircraft is soon speeding towards them. About 2,000,000 square miles are covered by the Royal Flying Doctor Service which operates from 14 bases.

Most homes in the outback have a two-way radio linking them to a base. When they need urgent help they simply call for it in much the same way as the city-dweller gets an ambulance.

Without such a service, life in the outback would mean constant dread of illness or injury, just as it did before 1927.

It was the vision and energy of a Presbyterian missionary that created the service, and the ingenuity of a young electrical engineer that helped to make it possible. The missionary saw that aircraft could be used to bring help quickly. The engineer conceived a simple two-way radio that almost anyone could operate.

This missionary was Dr. John Flynn, born in 1880, at Moliagul, in Victoria. In 1911, when he was ordained, he took charge of the Mission at Beltana, in arid country to the north of Adelaide. Here he first came to grips with the lonely interior.

Flynn travelled widely through Northern Territory, South Australia, Queensland and Western Australia and soon became known as "Flynn of the Inland." He set up hospitals and nursing homes for the Mission. His missionaries went out to remote districts but they could not cancel out the fear of injury and the impossibility of getting a doctor.

So he dreamed of a flying doctor service that would cast a "mantle of safety" over the people of the outback. With the swift development of planes during the First World War this came nearer to realization.

Aircraft could now overcome distances, but how could they be summoned? Radio, then in its infancy, was the answer. Flynn interested Alfred Traeger, a young South Australian electrical engineer in his scheme, and they toured the outback together experimenting on small portable sets that Traeger made.

Traeger realized that the set would have to be light, easily repaired, and above all, simple to work without available electricity.

Eventually he came up with a remarkably simple device that used pedals to generate the power needed.

This pedal-radio was to prove one of the great contributions to inland development. It removed the last obstacle to Flynn's dream, and solidly backed by the Australian Inland Mission, money was found to establish the first base at Cloncurry in Queensland.

Then Dr. St. Vincent Welsh was selected to become the world's first full-time flying doctor, making his pioneer flights in 1928 in a tiny De Havilland plane called "Victory." At the controls was Arthur Affleck, a pilot with Qantas, the newly formed bush airline.

So it began at Cloncurry, turning in a few years to a vast organization administered by the Australian Aerial Medical Service, and in 1953 Queen Elizabeth II granted use of the prefix, Royal.

Today the service has 14 bases linked by two-way radio with 1,000 outposts.

SCHOOLS OF THE AIR

These radio networks have many other uses apart from medical calls. Modern transceivers having replaced the old pedal-radios have made possible new Schools of the Air.

These schools supplement correspondence lessons sent out to children between the ages of five and fourteen who live beyond the reach of schools.

Specially trained teachers staff these Schools of the Air and so popular have they become and so great are their demands on radio time, there may soon be separate communication lines for them.

The effect on the lives of isolated, lonely children has been dramatic. The children soon lose their microphone shyness and get to know each other although hundreds of miles apart.

In off-peak hours the networks are put to good use for exchanging gossip and news, much as city dwellers use their telephones, with the one difference that everyone can listen in and no one resents this lack of privacy.

Yet in spreading Flynn's "mantle of safety" too little credit has been given to the skill of the pilots who fly these ambulance aircraft. They have few radio aids, sometimes none at all. There are no beams or beacons outback. Navigation depends on a personal knowledge

A bush pilot is always ready to bring aid to the remote parts of the country. An area in the Northern Territory of 524,000 square miles is covered by this service.

Our
NATIONAL HERO
BERT HINKLER
Left England
Feb. 7, 1928
Arrived Australia
Feb. 22, 1928
16 DAYS
A Good Australian
who holds a
World's Record

Bert Hinkler was one of the pioneer fliers, with Charles Kingsford-Smith, who flew from San Francisco to Brisbane in 1928. His plane was the "Southern Cross."

THE ARTS

With A. B. Paterson, the author of "The Man from Snowy River" and "Waltzing Matilda" which almost every schoolchild can recite, and Henry Lawson, the excellent short story writer, three more names will always be associated with Australia: Marcus Clarke, who wrote when he was only twenty-four, "For The Term of His Natural Life," a book on the penal colony in Tasmania; Mrs. Aeneus Gunn, "We of the Never-Never;" and Henry Handel Richardson, a woman writing under a pen name, who wrote her remarkable work "The

Helena Rubinstein, later Princess Gourielli, arrived in Melbourne as a girl in 1902 and became a pioneer in cosmetics and the care of the skin. She opened her first "salon de beauté" there at the age of 18 and it became an immediate success. Madame, as she was always called, established salons in 100 countries before her death in 1965.

of the country, instinct and a careful watch on the fuel tanks.

It is not easy at times to find a tiny pinpoint on some featureless landscape; one tin roof in the middle of a bare and everlasting plain; some ragged line of timber half lost in dust haze; the fine thread of a boundary fence; a water-hole among the sandhills; a sun-baked claypan that does duty as a landing strip. At night, landings might be made with the headlights of cars focussed on a roughly made strip, across the stumps of newly felled trees.

Viscount Dunrossil, a former Governor-General said: "This wonderful service, a combination of medical, aeronautical and radio skill and enterprise that leaps over distances, brings a really Australian answer, idealistic but practical, to an Australian problem."

Joan Sutherland left Australia to study operatic singing in London. Fourteen years later she returned, one of the most celebrated sopranos in the world, to sing the rôle of Lucia in "Lucia di Lammermoor" in Melbourne before touring Australia. So great was her success in Europe that the Italians called her La Stupenda!

Dame Nellie Melba, the great soprano, who trained for her operatic career in Paris, possessed a truly golden voice. She sang at Covent Garden in London and the Metropolitan Opera House in New York. Born Helen Mitchell, she took a stage name from her own city, Melbourne, and left Melba Hall there to perpetuate her name.

What is this? Are these the billowing sails of a ship? No. It is the Sydney Opera House at Benelong Point which will be completed in 1972, if more funds can be obtained by public lottery. It was designed by the Danish architect Joern Utzon to be the permanent home of the Sydney Symphony Orchestra.

The actor, Peter Finch, in the rôle of Aaron Stein, in the film, "Judith."

Fortunes of Richard Mahoney" in three volumes: "Australia Felix" (1913), "The Way Home" (1925) and "Ultima Thule" (1929).

Newer voices in Australian literature are Alan Morehead, Christopher Brennan, Patrick White, Gavin Casey and Judith Wright.

Two authors who have written outstanding plays are Catherine Duncan, "Song of the Morning," set in Crete during the evacuation of the Australian troops, and Ray Lawler, "The Summer of the Seventeenth Doll" about workers in the canefields.

While Australia has given birth to many well-known actors and actresses—Judith Anderson, Peter Finch, Cyril Ritchard, Dick Bentley, Diane Cilento—the theatre in Australia is undeveloped, and they have all had to win their spurs abroad.

Film actors include Errol Flynn, Merle Oberon, Ron Randell and Cecil Kellaway, who made their name in Hollywood.

The ballet has produced the versatile Robert Helpmann, who toured with Pavlova's company before joining the Sadler's Wells Ballet in London. He is now a Shakespearean actor and director. "Corroboree," an Australian ballet, was written by John Antill.

While a truly Australian school of painting has not yet been produced, the country can claim many able painters. Tom Roberts and Charles Conder belong to the early school. Will Dyson and the works of the four Lindsay brothers, Norman, Lionel, Percy and Daryl hang in several overseas galleries. New painters include Russel Drysdale, Sidney Nolan and William Dobell; and a group of aborigines headed by the late Albert Namatjira (who use water paints) have attracted much attention. Sculpture is well represented by Bertram Mackennal, Lyndon Dadswell and Tom Bass.

After Eileen Joyce, the pianist, the composer, Percy Grainger, and Gilbert Murray, the Greek scholar, it is perhaps in singers that the Australians have excelled. This "land of the songless birds" has produced Nellie Melba, Peter Dawson, Florence Austral, Joan Hammond, Kenneth Neate and Joan Sutherland.

LANGUAGE

Since the first landings at Botany Bay, Australia has developed its own distinctive language.

Degrees are conferred at Wilson Hall at the University of Melbourne.

This copper-covered dome, resting on arches set in a moat, is the headquarters of the Australian Academy of Science in Canberra.

The aboriginal words that came into use after the Blue Mountains were breached in 1813 were *boomerang, kangaroo, koala, kookaburra, gin,* an aboriginal woman. Then came *stock-*

The well-planned reading room at the Melbourne Public Library as it is seen from a fourth-floor gallery underneath the dome.

In Melbourne four denominational colleges are built in a half-circle round College Crescent. Ormond College (above), founded by the Presbyterian Church, like the others, covers an area of 10 acres.

The foundation stone of St. James' Church in Sydney was laid in 1819. It was originally intended as a courthouse, but the convict architect, Francis Howard Greenway, who played such a notable part in the planning of Sydney, was asked to turn it into a church. The graceful Georgian structure that he finished is still regarded as one of the finest buildings in the city. St. James' was dedicated in 1824.

The mission church at Groote Eylandt, the largest island in the Gulf of Carpentaria, is roofed in corrugated iron. Groote Eylandt, discovered by the early Dutch navigators, is now an aboriginal reservation.

yard, station, a farm, *gully,* a ravine, *overlander, jackaroo,* a new man on the station. From the aborigines, too, came *coo-ee,* to call, *corroboree,* a dance, *dingo,* a native dog, and *coolibah, yarrah* and *mulga* trees.

With the sheep and cattle stations well established came *wool-barber,* shearer, *ringer,* a stockman, *poddy-dodger,* one who steals unbranded calves, *bluey,* a type of cattle dog, and *bullocky,* driver of a bullock cart. From the mines we get *digger* and *fossicker,* one who digs and searches for gold.

Also from the bush we have *damper,* bread made from flour and water, and *Buckley's chance,* no chance at all. From *cockatoo farmer* we get *cocky; cane-cocky,* a grower of sugar cane.

Land hunger produced *way out, back-of-beyond, back of Bourke,* and *west of sunset.* The *swag* or *bluey* was so-called because the swagman's blanket was usually blue.

Other words still in use are *dinkum* or *fair dinkum!* true! *good-oh!* and *too right! Pull your head in* means mind your own business; *have a bash at,* make an attempt.

Even the winds have names: *willy-willy,* a fierce inland squall, *southerly buster,* a southerly gale, *Fremantle doctor,* the sea wind at Perth that lowers the temperature after a hot day.

Wonk is a "bush viol" or bass viol made from a tea chest, a sapling and stout fishing line; *Sheila* is a girl friend, *wowser,* a kill-joy, *whacko!* good! *You beaut!* shows approval or irony, and *stop your laughing* means stop making a fuss.

Big surf and an occasional shark are two of the hazards which do not prevent anyone who can swim plunging into the sea. Life-saving teams are stationed on all the beaches. Here at Collaroy Beach a surfboard race is starting. The contestants paddle furiously through the first line of breakers to deep water where they turn round a buoy and ride back to the beach.

In a Test Match between Australia and the West Indies at Sydney, the West Indian batsman, Seymour Nurse, is being caught out by the slip, Bobby Simpson. Gloves are only used by the batsman and the wicket-keeper.

Sailing is a popular pastime in the waters around Sydney. Here a race is about to begin.

It is perhaps in sport that the Australian is most outstanding, in tennis, golf, surfing, swimming, sailing, rowing, fishing, riding and horse racing. Besides rugby football, soccer has become popular since the post-war arrival of New Australians from Europe. Australia, too, is the land of bowls played on grass and, of course, of cricket. The most famous cricketer of all, Don Bradman, was knighted for his services.

The Australians, it would seem from this, love the out-of-doors and they will go, at the drop of a hat, on a picnic, the most famous and beloved of all being the hot midsummer Christmas Day picnic under the shade of some gums or within sound of the surf. Yet, while

Keith Miller, now retired, was a brilliant all-rounder. Cricket matches between Australia and England have been going on for a long time. In 1882, after a crushing Australian victory, someone said that English cricket was dead and that its ashes could now be carried to Australia. Since then, the Ashes have remained the symbol of victory in the Tests between the two countries.

Roy Emerson, Wimbledon champion and Australian Davis Cup star, races to return a forehand drive during the delayed final of the 1966 Victorian State Tennis Championships.

Ron Clarke, Olympic champion long-distance runner, doing road work near his home in a Melbourne suburb.

the theatre has been slow to get a toe-hold in Australia, when the Boyd Neel Chamber Orchestra toured the outback a few years ago, squatters and their families, stockmen and hands, rode hundreds of miles to hear them play Mozart and Scarlatti.

Yes, it is sitting on a fence chyacking (kidding) or leaning against a wall (they are great leaners) that we see the Australian most characteristically with his quiet, accented voice rising to end his sentences, eyes narrowed against the sun, ears out (Australians' ears do tend to stick out) to hear the sound of the postman crossing the dry gully on his way to the homestead . . . "Here he comes! Start the tea, someone!" and so the billy boils.

TOURISM

When visitors come to Australia, one of the first places they want to see is the Great Barrier Reef on the tropical coast of Queensland.

Yet Australia has many other lures: the Blue Mountains and the Jenolan limestone caves; the

miles of beaches along the Gold Coast with surf breaking; a trip round Tasmania's apple orchards and neat hedgerows; and for the adventurous a voyage to the interior to see Ayers Rock or the aboriginal reservations at Groote Eylandt, in the Gulf of Carpentaria. Or they can simply stay in Sydney and hear the laughing kookaburra at the Zoo. He's a real Aussie—fair dinkum!

Dawn Fraser, Olympic champion, holds 5 women's world swimming records. However, after the games held in Tokyo in 1964, she was banned from competition.

Australia's coat of arms was granted in 1912 by King George V. On the left is a kangaroo and on the right an emu, supporting a shield. Around the base are branches of wattle or mimosa.

4. GOVERNMENT

FEDERATION

ONE HUNDRED YEARS after the first settling of Australia, the six colonies, New South Wales, Victoria, Queensland, South and Western Australia with Tasmania, raised the problems of common defence, inter-colonial tariffs and immigration.

In 1891, under Henry Parkes, the Premier of New South Wales, an Australian Federal Convention was held, and of this, Sir Ernest Scott, the Australian historian writes:

"Rarely has federation been achieved except under external pressures or internal eruptions. Australia, however, had never known war. It was safe from outside aggression, protected by the Imperial Navy. It was brought to federation by sound political appreciation of the disabilities of disunion . . . Australian democracy chose its own men from its own ranks, nearly all of whom were native-born and schooled in their own land."

Opening of the First Federal Parliament in May, 1901, by the Duke of Cornwall and York, later King George V, is shown in this painting by Tom Roberts. His wife, later Queen Mary, stands behind him with the first Governor-General, the Earl of Hopetoun, and Sir Edmund Barton, the Prime Minister. Queen Victoria's crown, symbol of sovereignty, hangs above the platform.

COMMONWEALTH

The Commonwealth of Australia was declared to have come into being on January 1, 1901, by a proclamation issued by Queen Victoria. This historic announcement came after the Commonwealth Bill had passed both Houses of the Imperial Parliament.

The Governor-General of Australia, the Earl of Hopetoun, convened the first parliament of the Commonwealth in the same year.

The word "Commonwealth" was suggested by Henry Parkes in 1891 and gained general approval after Edmund Barton, Australia's first Prime Minister, showed what a fitting word it was.

"Commonwealth," he said, "is the grandest and most stately name by which a great association of self-governing people can be characterised."

CAPITAL

After some manoeuvring between the States of New South Wales and Victoria, as to where the Federal Capital should be, a separate Capital Territory was created on a grant of land between their borders to be called Canberra (pronounced CANb'ra). The First Federal Parliament to meet there was opened by the Duke of York in 1927.

CONSTITUTION

The Constitution, which the Australian people agreed on, and the United Kingdom Parliament enacted to create the Commonwealth, provided a Federal structure, the national level of government consisting of Crown, Parliament and Judiciary.

Thus Queen Elizabeth II is the Queen of

As part of his training as future head of the Commonwealth Prince Charles attended Timbertop, a branch of Geelong Grammar School, in Victoria. Here he is seen on the attractive, wooded campus.

Australia, and is the symbol of the association of members of the British Commonwealth of Nations. The Queen is represented in Australia by the Governor-General, and the Governors of the six States.

THE POLITICAL EDIFICE

The system of government in both Federal and State parliaments is modelled on the British cabinet system. Voters choose between candidates at free elections every three years.

Sir Robert Menzies set a record by serving as Prime Minister for 16 years.

John Grey Gorton, a member of the Liberal Party, became Prime Minister in 1968.

Federal Parliament House at Canberra, the capital city of Australia. When the six Australian states federated in 1901 a special area was set aside on the southeastern tablelands between New South Wales and Victoria, and an architect from Chicago, Walter Burley Griffin, designed Canberra. The building of the city began in 1913.

The main political parties are Liberal, Labour and Country.

The present Liberal Party is the youngest of the parties and was formed in 1944. Its main objective is: the maintenance of an intelligent, free and liberal democracy.

The Labour Party has been in existence since 1891 and claims the right to speak for organized workers, and is the chosen political instrument for most of the unions.

The Country Party dates from 1918 and represents the interests of graziers, farmers and horticulturalists. It demands decentralization and guaranteed prices for primary products.

A coalition Liberal-Country Government has been in office since 1949, following the defeat of the Chifley Labour Government.

The Lord Mayor of Melbourne, elected by 33 City Councillors, wears these ceremonial robes.

5. ECONOMY

The heart of Sydney has been dramatically changed by the erection of many new skyscrapers. The tall buildings symbolize the boom in Australia's economy, as the nation enters the 1970's with a broader range of industry than ever before.

AUSTRALIA has principally been an agricultural country, and for many years after the first settlement, all activities were concentrated on the land, particularly on sheep-farming, which is still Australia's largest rural industry. With 120,000 holdings, the land supports 160,000,000 sheep, 76 per cent of them Merinos. The wool clip averages 9 lbs. a head and Australian wool provides 45 per cent of all wool entering into world trade. Japan is now the largest single buyer of raw wool.

In addition to lamb, mutton and sheepskins there are large exports of beef and dairy products, pigs and poultry.

Australia is one of the main wheat-exporting countries. Sugar, too, is a major export along with butter, cheese, and wine.

Irrigation from new dams will open up large areas of fertile country near the Torrens River in Queensland and the Ord River in Western Australia, where 30,000 acres of rich soil for cotton are being flooded. Many American cotton farmers from the state of Arizona have brought their experience to bear here and much U.S. capital has been invested.

Quite recently a mining boom of enormous proportions has struck Western Australia with the vast iron deposits discovered in the desolate mountains or plateaus of Pilbara, 1,000 miles north of Perth. Five international mining concerns have concessions to terrain here and have contracted to supply Japanese steel companies with hundreds of millions of tons of raw and pelletized ore over the next two decades. By 1975, Australia expects to be the fourth largest exporter of iron ore. When mines, railways and ports are ready to send out this ore it will be at the rate of one ship a day.

Australia produces almost all the rutile of the non-Communist world. Rutile, the ore from which the strategic metal titanium is obtained, is now an important export item, along with copper, lead, zinc and manganese.

The recent discovery of rich deposits of

Inside the shed the shearing begins. The average weight of a fleece is nine pounds. Sheep are run in all States under wide changes of climate in three different regions: the Pastoral Zone, the Wheat-Sheep Zone and the High Rainfall Zone.

Broome, on the tropical north coast of Western Australia, is famous for pearls and pearl shell. The splendid "Star of the West" pearl was fished up by a Broome lugger in 1917. The pearling fleets fish the pearl beds from March to December, then lay-up for the cyclone season. Each lugger carries a crew of 8 or 9, including 2 divers.

This Deep Space Probe is part of the U.S. installation at Woomera Rocket Range for the tracking of space vehicles. Woomera is staffed by Australian scientists. On the left is part of the mobile crane used for servicing the "Dish," as the probe is called.

Newcastle, in New South Wales, draws its strength from steel mills, coal mining, and as a port for the fertile Hunter Valley and its produce—dairy, cattle, wine, wool, vegetables and maize.

bauxite, a source of aluminium, in the Gove Peninsula of the Northern Territory, is giving rise to a new town, Nhulunbury, which will be completely air-conditioned—a necessity in the very hot climate of the region. At the tip of Queensland's Cape York Peninsula, another new bauxite town, Weipa, has sprung up.

While tobacco is still a relatively small industry, Australia's wide climatic variations produce an enormous range of fruit for canning, bottling and drying.

Manufacturing, however, has now increased sharply, and employs more than a third of the

whole work force. Factories are producing diesel-electric locomotives, motor vehicles, earth-moving equipment, roller bearings, paper, cathode ray tubes, synthetic fibres, plastics and petroleum products.

The sources of power are coal, hydro-power and oil, coal and oil providing 72 per cent of

Australian vineyards are mostly small family concerns planted with vines brought from Europe when the country was first settled. Chateau Tahbilk, on the many bends of the Goulburn River near Melbourne, presses its grapes according to age-old custom. Many New Australians, including this lady who once owned a small vineyard in Reggio, in southern Italy, have settled here. She and her husband have found their way of life very little changed.

Australia's own car, the Holden, passing the assembly line at General Motors-Holden plant at Dandenong, Victoria.

all electrical energy. But the Snowy Mountain Scheme and the Torrens Island Power Station near Port Adelaide will change this picture.

By 1970, Australia was exporting manufactured goods to countries from which it had once imported the same items. Biggest of all customers is Japan, which draws most of its raw materials from Australia. One hindrance to expansion, however, has been a shortage of workers, in spite of the hordes of immigrants who have come in in recent years. Nonetheless, Australia's balance of payments show a surplus, which means that the country makes more money on its exports than it pays for its imports.

Bales of wool being loaded at Fremantle in Western Australia, aboard a Dutch ship bound for Genoa.